AF256419

Contents

Features...2

Stages of Development 4

Standards 5

Language Arts
Left to Right and Top to
  Bottom..................................6
Diagonal Lines and Circles 7
Above and Below 8
On, Off, In, and Out..................9
Letter *Mm*..............................10
Letter *Dd*...............................11
Letter *Ff* 12
Letter *Gg* 13
Letter *Bb* 14
Letter *Tt*................................15
Letter *Ss* 16
Letter *Ww* 17
Letter *Kk* 18
Letter *Jj* 19
Letter *Pp* 20
Letter *Nn* 21
Letter *Cc* 22
Letter *Hh* 23
Letter *Ll* 24
Letter *Rr* 25
Letter *Vv*...............................26
Letter *Yy* 27
Letter *Zz* 28
Letter *Qq* 29
Letter *Xx*...............................30
Letter *Aa* 31
Letter *Oo* 32
Letter *Ii* 33
Letter *Uu* 34
Letter *Ee*...............................35
Partner Letters..........................36
Alphabet Order.........................37
Same Beginning Sounds 38
Rhyming Words 39

Math
Top, Middle, and Bottom 40
Before, After, and Between......41
Same Size.................................42

Same Color...............................43
Same Shape 44
Differences 45
Circles 46
Rectangles 47
Triangles..................................48
Squares 49
Number *1* 50
Number *2* 51
Number *3* 52
Number *4* 53
Number *5* 54
Review Numbers *1–5* 55
Number *6* 56
Number *7* 57
Number *8* 58
Number *9* 59
Number *10*...............................60
Review Numbers *6–10* 61
Review Numbers *1–10* 62
Equal Groups 63
Fewer.......................................64
More...65
Order Numbers to 10................66
Long and Short.........................67
Big and Little 68
Hot and Cold 69
Heavy and Light 70
Patterns....................................71
Ordinal Numbers......................72
Classify....................................73

Science
Living and Nonliving Things...74
Needs of Living Things 75
Living Things Grow.................76
Many Kinds of Animals 77
Where Animals Live 78
Parts That Help Animals 79
Parts That Help Animals Stay
  Safe..80
Ways That Animals Move........81
Many Kinds of Plants 82
Plant Parts 83
Seeds 84
Resources 85

Parts of the Human Body.........86
Senses......................................87
Humans Grow and Change 88
Healthy Foods 89
Exercise...................................90
Staying Healthy 91
Emergency Numbers 92
Natural or Man-made...............93
Classify Materials 94
Weather 95
Seasons....................................96
Night and Day 97
Earth's Surface 98
Resources Are Useful...............99
Conserve Resources 100
Characteristics of Magnets.....101
Characteristics of Air 102
Gravity 103

Social Studies
Left and Right 104
Near and Far 105
Families Do Things
  Together...............................106
Families Are Different 107
Families Celebrate.................108
Countries and Their Flags.....109
People Have Needs................110
Needs and Wants 111
Coins 112
Count Pennies 113
People in the Community.......114
Tools People Use 115
Stores in the Community 116
Places to Work and Live 117
Understanding Maps 118
Use a Map 119
Rules......................................120
Signs......................................121
Good Citizens........................122
Where People Work 123
Kinds of Jobs.........................124
Transportation 125
Roads.....................................126
Technology 127
Past and Present 128

Features

These Skills Are Presented in Various Ways Throughout *3-2-1 Learn* for Ages 4–5

- Traces lines, shapes, numbers, and letter formations
- Counts objects
- Uses positional words such as *on*, *off*, *in*, *out*
- Compares sizes, shapes, and quantities
- Sorts and classifies objects
- Matches letters
- Names body parts
- Identifies some capital and lowercase letters
- Retells information

ACTIVITIES IN THIS BOOK ARE PRESENTED BY THE SUBJECT AREAS OF LANGUAGE ARTS, MATH, SCIENCE, AND SOCIAL STUDIES.

Pages in the Language Arts Section Provide:

- Tracing letter formations
- Naming capital and lowercase letters of the alphabet
- Practice holding writing tools correctly
- Making letter-sound associations
- Identifying letters in written context

Pages in the Math Section Provide:

- Positional words
- Naming and tracing shapes
- Naming and writing numbers
- Counting
- Classifying
- Measuring
- Patterning

Features
3-2-1 Learn, SV 9781419099281